To Bob, who... I
love deeply always.

Judy

June, 1968

I MARRY YOU

I MARRY YOU

A Sheaf of Love Poems

John Ciardi

RUTGERS UNIVERSITY PRESS

New Brunswick, New Jersey

MANUFACTURED IN THE UNITED STATES OF AMERICA

DESIGNED BY ANDOR BRAUN

Men Marry What They Need. I Marry You

Men marry what they need. I marry you,
morning by morning, day by day, night by night,
and every marriage makes this marriage new.

In the broken name of heaven, in the light
that shatters granite, by the spitting shore,
in air that leaps and wobbles like a kite,

I marry you from time and a great door
is shut and stays shut against wind, sea, stone,
sunburst, and heavenfall. And home once more

inside our walls of skin and struts of bone,
man-woman, woman-man, and each the other,
I marry you by all dark and all dawn

and learn to let time spend. Why should I bother
the flies about me? Let them buzz and do.
Men marry their queen, their daughter, or their mother

by names they prove, but that thin buzz whines through:
when reason falls to reasons, cause is true.
Men marry what they need. I marry you.

Contents

I MARRY YOU

Snowy Heron

What lifts the heron leaning on the air
I praise without a name. A crouch, a flare,
a long stroke through the cumulus of trees,
a shaped thought at the sky—then gone. O *rare!*
Saint Francis, being happiest on his knees,
would have cried *Father!* Cry anything you please.

But praise. By any name or none. But praise
the white original burst that lights
the heron on his two soft kissing kites.
When saints praise heaven lit by doves and rays,
I sit by pond scums till the air recites
Its heron back. And doubt all else. But praise.

Epithalamion After a War

Now by a ritual of legality
You are my flesh's darling, my mind's encounter,
And every nearness has propriety
Approved by clergy, clerk, and editor.
By the civil law's instinct for procreation
Our blood has other license than the moon.

Still in all our carnival of clouds,
Our languid wakings and pajamaed noons,
Shed boys in bone-rims watch us from their clods,
Shod boys on warheads practice dropping suns,
And Law that lets us be till Law arrives
Talks to itself, a jargon round our lives.

My hand, the cunning heirloom of the ape,
That fumbled at the ring of ritual,
Bringing the finger of propriety up
To ceremony's civil spectacle,
Worked the sere sickle finger of a gun
And closed on fire when Law's last word was spoken.

And held a stick that stirred a heap of bones
From which rats leaped like Morse in their own code:
"I loved you, darling, in organic banns
But an intruder tips our reeking bed
Who has no instinct for our native sex
But a confusion of hybrid intellects."

4

But spill your flowers, my darling, as they burst
Golden from the great stem, and, spendthrift sure,
Spin our your five wits followed from the first
By bones beyond the Law. There is no more
Than man and woman, shedding as they go,
And faster in their blood than Law is slow.

To Judith Asleep

My dear, darkened in sleep, turned from the moon
that riots on curtain-stir with every breeze,
leaping in moths of light across your back . . .
far off, then soft and sudden as petals shower
down from wired roses—silently, all at once—
you turn, abandoned and naked, all let down
in ferny streams of sleep and petaled thighs
rippling into my flesh's buzzing garden.

Far and familiar your body's myth-map lights,
traveled by moon and dapple. Sagas were curved
like scimitars to your hips. The raiders' ships
all sailed to your one port. And watchfires burned
your image on the hills. Sweetly you drown
male centuries in your chiaroscuro tide
of breast and breath. And all my memory's shores
you frighten perfectly, washed familiar and far.

Ritual wars have climbed your shadowed flank
where bravos dreaming of fair women tore
rock out of rock to have your cities down
in loot of hearths and trophies of desire.
And desert monks have fought your image back
in a hysteria of mad skeletons.
Bravo and monk (the heads and tails of love)
I stand, a spinning coin of wish and dread,

counting our life, our chairs, our books and walls,
our clock whose radium eye and insect voice
owns all our light and shade, and your white shell

spiraled in moonlight on the bed's white beach;
thinking, I might press you to my ear
and all your coils fall out in sounds of surf
washing a mystery sudden as you are
a light on light in light beyond the light.

Child, child, and making legend of my wish
fastened alive into your naked sprawl—
stir once to stop my fear and miser's panic
that time shall have you last and legendry
undress to old bones from its moon brocade.
Yet sleep and keep our prime of time alive
before that death of legend. My dear of all

saga and century, sleep in familiar-far.
Time still must tick *this is, I am, we are.*

Morning: I Know Perfectly How in a Minute
You Will Stretch and Smile

As pilots pay attention to the air
> lounging on triggers wired into their ease;
> seeing what they do not see, because their eyes
> are separate cells; hearing what they do not hear,
> because a life is listening in their place;
> and so with their five senses and a sixth
> cocked to their element, free and transfixed,
> slouch as they hurtle, ticking as they laze—

so in the mastered master element
> love is or nothing, silences unheard,
> flickerings unseen, and every balancing
> and tremor of our senses still unsensed,
> joins and enjoins, and, nothing left to chance,
> spins our precisions in us as we nod.

Sometimes the Foundering Fury

Sometimes the foundering fury that directs
the prayer through storm, the sucking mouth;
sometimes a gentleness like a parent sex;
sometimes an aimless tasting mild as broth

or the drugged eye of the invalid; sometimes
a naked arm laid loose along the grass
to the brown-eyed breast and the great terms
of the turning flank printed by root and moss;

sometimes a country in a white bird's eye
coasting the shells of cities in their past,
the roads that stretch to nothing but away,
a horseman wandering in his own dust—

say you were beautiful those years ago,
flush as the honey-blonde who rode the shell
in Sandro Botticelli's studio,
and what we are now, we were then,

and lost, and found again—what shall we wish
to visit from ourselves against that death
but their imagination on our flesh?
There is no other body in all myth.

The Stills and Rapids of Your Nakedness

The stills and rapids of your nakedness
in the bird-started morning mist of sun
spill from my sleep like April's waking rush
into the groundswell and green push of May.

All days tell this. Season and season, this.
This apple to my mind's eye. This new bread.
This well of living water where the bell
of heaven is. This home's door and first kiss.

Darling, to see your eyes when you, too, stir,
turn all their inner weathers to a smile
I write you this: a jargon in the sky
twitters about your sleep; and like a churning

the dawn beats into gold; and, like a field
the wind turns over, all your body lives
its circling blood; and like the first of leaves,
I start from wood to praise you and grow green.

The Deaths about You When You Stir in Sleep

The deaths about you when you stir in sleep
hasten me toward you. Out of the bitter mouth
that sours the dark, I sigh for what we are
who heave our vines of blood against the air.

Old men have touched their dreaming to their hearts:
that is their age. I touch the moment's dream
and shrink like them into the thing we are
who drag our sleeps behind us like a fear.

Murderers have prayed their victims to escape,
then killed because they stayed. In murdering time
I think of rescues from the thing we are
who cannot slip one midnight from the year.

Scholars have sunk their eyes in penitence
for sins themselves invented. Sick as Faust,
I trade with devils, damning what we are
who walk our dreams out on a leaning tower.

Saints on their swollen knees have banged at death:
it opened: they fell still. I bang at life
to knock the walls away from what we are
who raise our deaths about us when we stir.

Lovers unfevering sonnets from their blood
have burned with patience, laboring to make fast
one blood-beat of the bursting thing we are.
I have no time. I love you by despair.

Till on the midnight of the thing we are
the deaths that nod about us when we stir,
wake and become. Once past that fitful hour,
our best will be to dream of what we were.

Looking over the Rail of Ponte Sant' Angelo as a Guide Goes By with His Flock in Trail

What the Roman sun says to the Romans
    (a boy fishing the Tiber with a seine
    while two old men and a stone saint watch from the
      bridge
    that leads to Castel Sant' Angelo, where once
    a cypress forest mourned across the roof
    for a faded emperor gone like his forest
    into the stonework)
                what the Roman sun
    ("a species of tumulus or burial mound
    as for example pyramids cairns barrows
    and similar monuments common to many cultures")
    says to the Romans ("the stone structure
    visible to us being simply the base")
    I have said to you in all the tongues of sleep.

I Look through My Dead Friend's
Eyes at the House of Love

I look through my dead friend's eyes at the house of love:
plaster scabs from lath, windows break out
in toothy gapes, doors stagger from their pins.
See what a feast this is, my love, my love,
our shelves of mouse turds, dusts, and dirty damps!

I try this vision on like the wrong glasses
and every straightness quivers to a blur,
and every surface whorls to drink me in.
Well then, this is a world for twisted eyes.
Or if my eye offend me I'll pluck it out.

And still be chanceled in our breathing bed,
the dusk behind the taper and the cup,
as I was once—a holy man, though I lost
my holy ghost, my terror, and my sin
when I had got my own death down by heart.

And there's no nonsense like it. If I forgive
that death, I lose my last prayer. Let us live.

Black snow, the winter's excrement
on the foul street, thaws
oil-slick puddles traffic-splashed
back on black snow. Spring
begins its rumor everywhere,
a new critique and weather.
The ripple is running under
the river's rotting ice,
the winter-lock jaws open.
There is no sun. Only a gray day
warmer than most.
               Warmer than most,
colder than some, I mail
three letters at the corner, turn
on black slush skirting puddles,
shy from traffic splash, wade
the unclean graves of winter,
drift-dregs of dead accumulation.
The first corpse is beerbottle green,
a honeycomb of filth on glass.
What's dirty passes. And returns.
What's clean . . .
             What's clean! My dirty death,
my death to walk on, rehearses
days in a rotting season. Love—
the pulse in a skin glove. Time—
a civic trash on Spring's groundswell. The Scene—
Hellgate at the glacial recession,
flower faces of children in red hats
already wanton in water, splashing   *15*

oil-slick puddles on the black snow,
a mother scolding from a window.

From a window
you smile, and I,
having mailed three promises
to the fiction of a world,
return through these real Limbos
balancing a bubble of myself
that shines, and is surprised it does not break.

"Look!" you said. "Look!"

On Easter morning two egrets
flew up the Shrewsbury River
between Highlands and Sea Bright

like two white hands
washing one another
in the prime of light.

Oh lemons and bells of light,
rails, rays, waterfalls, ices—
as high as the eye dizzies

into the whirled confetti
and rhinestones of the breaking blue
grain of lit heaven,

the white stroke of the egrets
turned the air—a prayer
and the idea of prayer.

A Thanks That Flesh Is Sad

The sad soft scars, childbitten
        from the rose-dust once of flesh,
        I kiss unhailed in my arms and sigh for.
        A thanks all lovers come to when they dare.

That you were sunblush lit as the writhen
        sprays of orchards in the rush of Spring,
        and swelled and softened as ever peach on its bough,
        an allegory of plenty on stilled air;

and that I laid my last tears in your breast
        like worms' eyes from the long sods of my death,
        and sang that sadness over in your arms
        till I outlived the white bone in its grave—

I rise past pity in a lust of praise
        for every loss that stores us. Scar by scar
        the dearest flesh is sad, and spins in man
        his rose of fire, the raging of his joys.

A black stallion and a white mare
are posed in the field nearest the road
as one enters the model farm.
Magnificent and sudden they are, and yet
too obviously of the rich farmer's pride;
too obviously matched and put just there
that no one might miss seeing them. And thus
not wholly nature, and not less than nature,
but an exploitation: true, but overmanaged.

I should not have invented them. Not surely
since Freud and the freudlings, real or posed,
parsed out the sample- and too-obvious-dream
the farmer, being obvious and illiterate,
sets up to be his name plate in this field.
I should not have invented them, and yet,
there they are centering the morning air,
and I walk past again to look at them,
too perfect to be likely or to avoid.

I watch *him:* a wound quiver of inner balances
built rippling to brute bulk: Greek head and neck,
bulwarked Arabian chest, haunches light-coiled
and rounded huge from all the wars of kings—
an ease awaiting its next chemistry.
As *she* waits in the swan arch of herself,
all dove white and all coiled and all at ease,
till he flame in the terror of his making
and she shake all the forests under him.

Three days ago I passed them in their storm,
clear as the kind of truth schools are about;
but every lesson lied, and the truth was
a bloodshock drummed, the air stampeded,
a black and a white energy crazed and rearing
with an agony like a lion on its backs,
from which real blood flowed black, unholdable, driven,
he to her battered ecstasy in pain, she
struck and still plunging to his battery.

And I saw watching from across the field
the rich farmer—too rich even to care
that nature is striped with injury—watching,
too obviously repaid by what he was not
to care for one scarred mare. Her coat would heal.
Would heal enough. And he had brutes enough
to waste these two perfections from the rest
of his manhandled teasers and iced sperm.
He wanted what he wanted in itself.

And if I saw his staging overstaged,
any man living could sneer back my lie
should I deny the sweats that broke in me,
the thud of self on self that beat afire
out of the night-thought of a whole illusion
where once, black stroke on white stroke, seized,
monstrous and inGodding, we reared from time.
Then burst apart, coiled down as they are now,
at ease till our next chemistry upon us.

What rich men can afford, others may still
stare at inside themselves. I have walked back
morning by morning to an energy
I need to touch again, rank with ourselves.
The white mare and black stallion strike their poses
into a memory that makes again
the world's well at the roots from which we sprang.
I hang upon the rail as on a limb
of the whole tree up through time, and watch again

original energy in its place below,
too obvious to invent or not to know.

The Deaths They Are, Those Great Eyes from the Air

The deaths they are, those great eyes from the air
like water-globes hung in their seven lights,
watch at all gardens, shedding dews of grace
when lovers most remember what to do.

Then slags burn mineral rainbows, ruins come caroling
out of their rake-teeth and sag, wrack
spumes far as the last keel's going, and time
shivers a tropic of bells and vibrations

in the blood of beginning again. What other pool
than the moon-flesh of lovers watched from their past
will change a star's reflection to a thought
that justifies the listening of the air?

It is my father drives me from his dust
among my bones' moon-arches, his and his,
and spins the whirlpool on my pole of flesh,
and spines the air with trellises of notes;

until I will your flesh to all their deaths,
and to all mine, and to the lives between,
in such a choir-burst as the season's are
under their dome of winds that stir your hair.

Most Like an Arch This Marriage

Most like an arch—an entrance which upholds
and shores the stone-crush up the air like lace.
Mass made idea, and idea held in place.
A lock in time. Inside half-heaven unfolds.

Most like an arch—two weaknesses that lean
into a strength. Two fallings become firm.
Two joined abeyances become a term
naming the fact that teaches fact to mean.

Not quite that? Not much less. World as it is,
what's strong and separate falters. All I do
at piling stone on stone apart from you
is roofless around nothing. Till we kiss

I am no more than upright and unset.
It is by falling in and in we make
the all-bearing point, for one another's sake,
in faultless failing, raised by our own weight.

The Stone without Edges Has Not Been Mined

The stone without edges has not been mined,
and the kiss that does not lie has not been joined.
Nothing falls from Heaven but of its weight.
       I love you of my loss.

What day begets the child of no nuisance?
In a tantrum after tenderness, for nothing,
I have slapped the child of our impudence.
       I love you of my shame.

Be old leather. Dry, as a hide in sun
cracks and turns dust and puffs at a touch,
once airborne pastes of life have smeared it.
       I love you of our death.

The bride without escapes has not been kissed,
nor the groom without terrors. Having dared
our own tears and a child's, we have our healing.
       I love you of that health.

For My Son John

Jonnel, this is for you — my river-saint-named
and first-born son, the lamb
for whom the prophets flamed their beards to God
and rolled their eyeballs inside out to praise.

Nothing so grand, so rank with twitching sweats
of holy rapture does
for the tousling hand across your mop-top. Oaf-cub! —
a long noise off from glory, but my own pup.

And glorious for all that. Spit on my lie
if ever I allow
the dry-hack of a wordless generation
to rack up in my throat and choke my praise

of that blazed glory-bed where, blood to blood,
man-beat and woman-beat,
like swollen pods lashed by a golden wind,
we burst you from our love into our love.

All men brag this. So let it praise all men.
The bed that bore you
was no garden but a nature, and there
the great man and great woman touched their tree.

Then when that great woman slowed and swelled,
a langorous long smile
grew in her eyes and mine, and the first thump
beat our two bellies at once where we lay locked.

Whatever glory spoke in those flame-bearded
God-knocked and goatherd deserts
whose gales blew through the prophets mouth-at-law;
or roars here in the speed-run of flag-extras—

this is for you, the son of praising man
up from the glory bed
in the weathers of the touched tree chosen.
The first life and the first and still the first.

Two Poems for Benn

i Romping

Silly. All giggles and ringlets and never
about to stop anything without fussing:
get down I say! Do you think I took your mother
to beget me a chimp for my shoulder?
I'm forty, boy, and no weight lifter.
Go find some energy your own size.
Get down! — Well, just once more.
There. Now get down, you baby-fat incubus.
Go ride your imagination. No, I don't care
how many kisses you'll write me a check for.
A million? Some banker you are. Still —
a million of anything is a lot of something.
All right. Once more, then. But just once. You hear?

ii Stopped Suddenly that He is Beautiful

It happens at once and unthought of: what bumbled zooms,
what clattered turns to speech, what sprawled
leaps and becomes a balance on the air.

It is an elegance beyond all choosing.
As an elk is sighted. As a partridge
explodes from under the hunter's foot.

As a porpoise breaks the surface like light.
As a pear tree one morning blooms, its scroll on scroll
tiered in the sun at perfect random — —

Yesterday you were all yolk and today
there are gulls in your laughter, and land and sea
in the light from you, and a name

in the measure of your eyes. Little boy, little boy,
I feel an absence beginning. You are touched already
by the shape of what you will be:

the stranger I go to my grave for and give my house to,
as once it came from a stranger stopped in love
to cry: "My son! My son! I am well traded!"

That Summer's Shore

On The Island, finding you naked and pearled
in a summer sea, and our daughter naked by you,
at froth with the universe and laughing a splendor
into the huff and sneeze-out of the swell—

finding you there, you two, by that most world
most spoken, saying from time
how we are inhaled and exhaled by a sound
between two water-heaves, I swore

to speak the deeps of the kiss of man and woman,
to say you as you are inside my breath
after the turning apart of arms from their twining,
in the night nest before sleep, yet truer than waking,

warm from your warmth, this man beside this woman,
all man beside all woman, at touch and Adamic.
I speak that nearness in the tongue of prayer,
seeing you distanced by sea that distances all,

yet naked as all touch of human nights
housed in their candle-breath above the huff,
my hand shaped into sleep across your hand
as anything in nature seeks its resting.

So, returning from the Mainland, I found you
there in the sea in your woman nakedness,
and the girl in her girl nakedness, and the sea
silken and long and breathing of our sleep.

Thigh-deep in water, you stood and waved,
the woman-pear of your body drawn full
to the left of your arm, and your breasts
flecked with prisms, and your fur with crystals.

And there at the lace-edge, ankle-splash-deep, the girl
ran chittering in her bud-roundness. She
was all peach and you were pear-and-almond,
your roundness slackened but sweeter for ripeness.

And in joy and in terror, I saw the sea
blink, and you were not there, and I was not there,
and the round girl had slackened to woman, and another
round girl ran chittering by the sea and was watched in love.

And I made this praise to your nakedness in the sea.

Ten Years Ago When I Played at Being Brave

Sleep was what deviled it. The days were easy.
The going itself was nothing—once in air
there was the next thing and the next to do.
We would come back or burn. Would or would not.
Whatever would happen was already going.

It was that sleep before—which was no sleep
but a long whisper: "By this time tomorrow
you may have burned."—"Well, and suppose I do:
what do I want tonight? If I could have it,
what's the last thing I really want forever?"

——I need to say this to you as it was.
As nearly as I can. What *could* a man want?
A woman, yes, but this was for perfections:
a last night on the Universe, and paid for.
I wanted Eve, her nightname of the blood.

——Then—in one moonquake—it was worlds ago.
Three thousand nights, and more, and numberless,
I've hailed your body's tropics from the moon
and sung your surfs out of my sleep, and come
to every Eve and nightname in my need.

This is to dream what thousand dead men bless you:
you were their one most reason not to die.
Were I where they have gone and could some dream
patch that torn sleep, I think I could make whole
the flesh of all wish in one dream of you.

I wake then—as I woke once to be born
out of their dark—locked to your rustling islands,
whole as a flood tide flowing to your shore,
a thousandth and a thousandth time again
come from the shapeless waters under time.

A Dawn Twelve Years After a War:
I Sit, the Children Sleep

Orion drowns away
south of the dawn.
Milked under by the day.
Not set, but gone.
Washed out still at half height
by the new stain of light.

Like snow by a campfire
light heaps the sill,
till, as the change rides higher
the colors run; a chill
first white, most like a mist,
freezes out amethyst.

My colors hid from light—
Myra, Jonnel, Benn—
stir, still in their night,
settle again,
and leave me where I was,
a pause inside a pause.

Last, Venus morning star
wanes out, a half-seen dot.
Strange, it was at war
I learned the skies, to plot
meridians unseen
but cable-taut between

darks and the blue-green rose
out of a bomber's belly,

time and the twinkle-toes
of tracers over Bali.
Through skylines like a net
continents rose and set

between my life and death.
Cities turned to noon
at midnight of the earth.
An arm waved out of stone:
"Goodbye from every deep.
Skies are not to keep."

Now Myra, Jonnel, Benn
stir in the keeping clock,
the stars wash out again,
and time strolls up the walk
between my two prize yews.
Goodmorning and good news.

Letter from an Empty House

The hour pings like a bird hatched from a bell
as I come in. And the last stroke is silence.
The house is a hoaxter's garden—all in glass:
not one leaf withered, banks and borders trim,
every stem gleaming like a flower—but flowerless.
Neat nothing. A lit emptiness on file.

"Well, come now," I begin, "a week, ten days,
two weeks at most . . . two weeks out of a year . . ."
I could count year by year how far I am
since midnight racked me sobbing on its moon,
and having you was more than I could stand,
and leaving you was more than I could stand.

And what if I *should* count? What could *that* change?
I shall not die of flames I lived in once.
But if I need fire less, I need warmth more.
I cannot stand this glassblown winter garden
without your summering colors, or the spring
and breakage of the children's insolence.

It is three days now and I am already
emptied. I have touched nothing. I come and go
like a bellhop through a suite. Even the ash trays
are polished bright as a doll's funeral.
Nobody lives here and nothing happens. I wait,
not wanting to go to bed, and then I go.

Say I am cranky with habit and middle age.
A not-much and no matter. It is as if

I had left my pulse in the next room, like glasses:
I cannot wholly breathe nor wholly see.
And though I put the light out, and my breath,
nothing turns off, and nothing falls in place.

I cannot sleep. My sleep is in your hand.
Until you touch me with it, I stare blind
into the waking dark. I cannot wake;
my waking is a stir that is not here—
a babble, and a tumble, and a yell
that ends in kisses, tears, or a new babble;

but is the tick and bell note of the house
whose one last bird pings in its egg downstairs,
and then again, and then again. I hear
the hours I cannot use fall and fall still.
I lie on absence, a white frozen moon,
and cannot sleep, and then at last I do.

i

How shall I reach you till I have imagined
    my first and last of days, and all days,
    turned and turning, that make and let us
    answer and reach for what we are of time?
    How shall I reach you till I have imagined?

Time sags in the middle. Our nights outrun us.
    All energy and impromptu, the flown children
    of our best, leap, strewing our pauses
    with clatters of their shining ignorance.
    How shall I reach you till I have imagined

earth as it is, world as we are—a sum
    of man and woman reached imagining?
    "I love you," says a tongue too Protestant
    for nights, too Catholic for days.
    And so with all men of this tongueless time

I can say nothing till I have imagined
    by long ways round the saying
    what part of what truth tells us as we are
    who reach, and think to reach. To truth?
    Truths are not spoken whole, nor all at once.

ii

An earth taste in the stay of love is first.
    Begun before itself. As earth was
    whose rains hissed striking centuries long into

37

hot original stone cups. A sea starting.
Millennia of steams to a first horizon

visible, and none to see it—an out-of-time.
    If there is time in the kiln, firing and cooling,
    the locked shapes do not keep
    it, but themselves. Shapes are
    not time but things. There is this earth

come from its kiln timeless, and a bird called
    through late fern-eras like a mountain-tide
    coming and going. Called: "There is this earth
    of shapes and shadowings. There is this earth,
    and who will think of it?" Till a man thought it.

It is to think his earth again as he
    in the arms of saber-tooth and woman learned
    and learned to stay his death, that I imagine
    what shapes out of what kiln have told
    the praising man his tongues, their first of birdsong.

iii

"There is this earth: what shall you think of it?"
    the bird sings his first dawn again from sleep's end;
    a sky leap into day. If that were all!
    Ah, if it were and every bird-sung hay
    a heaven of bounced angels!

If that were all! To hear the first-told name
    rung out of morning lungs and walk feasted

on sunburst dewdeeps—
taken and held by airy abundances
and armored against time by time!

I wake, and find you in the risen bird's
outpouring of the darks that store his song
for the washed apple-harvests of the light.
And ah, if that were all! If starting
were all there were of love!

iv

Time sags in the middle. Worlds outrun us.
Are worlds true? True as any. I have killed
airily over unknown towns to reach you,
setting my torch to the world for the world's
saying. May those deaths be.

I chose them, or there is no choice. There is—
this world and what shall lovers think of it
who think love is what chooses? There is this world
and once inside it, burning, true, I chose—
wholly as I choose love now—death.

Forgive me if you must, but I will be
forgiven only for what I am, who am
choiceless as any, waiting as I may
for a life to happen to me. As time sags.
Dreaming to reach you from a first-named need.

One strictness does for all, and love may say it.

v

One strictness does for all. As fat priests know
        how much they eat of what they do not marry,
        and still give up their starved souls to the host,
        I know what food it is that lets me be

part of a truth so strictly told it does
        to bring one dove down in the name of love.
        Come to your blowsy darling with the rose
        between his teeth, my love, and let him move

the one stone he can loosen with a prayer:
        to live in the world and be what a man is
        against his death, and nearest to your sleep.
        A tribesman of your body in his night.

vi

My ten red fingers which are each a boy
        close hot as rum. Whatever chucks a rump
        I praise a-cackle in the bounce of whee!

A god who laughs made wine. Let my boys work
        their shaggy time through mosses of the rose.
        I dance Frère Hèrcule's stick flung through the tree,

Rustico slugging the devil to pink Hell,
        Cunnegonde's jewel box. All that shakes a leg
        toward godsent Wives of Bath by Millers told

I raise a hoop for. If Pacelli can,
　　　　or Chaplain Ike, or Papa Poppycock,
　　　　tell them to tell God that I like His hay!

　　　vii

Then, dead and drawn, a quiver at your hip,
　　　　I am the solved man, regal and at ease
　　　　with all my species answered in your arms
　　　　and all my tribes in order in their caves
　　　　and all my names in place inside themselves.

The strictness is to be. To let our lives
　　　　out of our lives, and answer as they come
　　　　like dancers to the music, keeping whole
　　　　by changing when it changes. Or unchanged
　　　　but being one to one another's answers

in every motion outward of the sound.
　　　　I study toward perfection what I know
　　　　in perfect place already: that you are
　　　　what every reaching reaches. And returns.
　　　　Praising and praised, and all made visible.

What World It Is the Crocodile May Know

What world it is the crocodile may know
    Gorged in the rotten heavens of his mud,
Or swirling in white water on his cow
    Till every storm is second to his blood.

Or think how vultures out of Nature's mind
    Descend like rancid angels to their chicks
Bearing the carrion mercy on the wind
    From stinking bones to shelves of stinking sticks.

Spill. Spill. These jaws have splendor, these beaks grace.
    It is that world walked on by storms of light
I hold you in to hold my blood in place
    Till angels come to break me in the night.

Letter from a Death Bed

This afternoon, darling, when you were here,
I meant to say some true and final thing
and could not. I am not all myself
but a chemical changeling, a tide of salt and juices,
a shore from which I sink, wash back, and sink.

Then in a rhythm and for an interval
I am again. I know then—now—exactly
what was my best. That instant—this—I seize,
which is no memory but the being again. At last,
for this instant, I can say "I love you."

I have it here: that first night and the first
again, and always, incredibly—thank you—the first
from the instant of your turning, your dropped silks
a froth at your feet, and like a grained flame
the leap and repose of your nakedness in its giving.

Let the tide wash that from me if it can.
A dark like your body's fuzzes and crinkles takes me.
Then blanks. But is always the last of me.
The last of me going from me is you. And returns.
Goes and returns. Goes and returns. Holding you.

No, I am all going. All arrows set from the wind.
All out and away. Skewed only by cheer and nurses.
Damn them, I will die in my own climate.
What breath have I ever drawn from the wax-weathers
under their hothouse skulls and fogged windows?

I tend a refusal better than their prayers,
these flour-faced angels with their piano legs
who don't think I notice. Today that doctor,
his smile put on with adhesive tape, came poking:
He'll have me out of here in nothing flat.

I know damn well he will. Nothing and flat.
He wants to know my religion. "Refusal," I tell him.
"The Church of the First Covenant of Damned-if-I-Will."
Fool. Does he think what a man lives by
gets changed by his dying? Well, I'm cantankerous—

must I *like* dying to gossip?—Oh, I hear them:
"Twelve, he's a queer one. Won't be told what's wrong.
Just doesn't want to know." I know all right.
If they think what I'm dying of's any one thing,
they haven't healing enough to mend a rip.

. . . What was it I said? "Some true and final thing."
I meant a better end to that beginning.
Well, maybe cantankerousness is true and final.
—No. No, it isn't. Your eyes are true and final.
Your smile even in pity and enforced. Your hand . . .

Thank you for smiling, darling. Don't come back.
Come bury the bones. Come take away the clothes rack
they'll hang my tatters on. But the end's here.
This is my last stroke as myself. My going.
My meat has this last energy and no more—

to praise you as you are from all I leave.